Samplers
IN CROSS STITCH

Jane Alford

MEREHURST

The projects in this book were all stitched with DMC stranded cotton embroidery threads. The keys given with each chart also list thread combinations for those who wish to use Anchor or Madeira threads. It should be pointed out that the shades produced by different companies vary slightly, and it is not always possible to find identical colours in a different range.

Published in 1993 by Merehurst Limited
Ferry House, 51-57 Lacy Road, Putney, London SW15 1PR
Text & charts copyright © 1993 Jane Alford
Photography & illustrations copyright © 1993 Merehurst Limited
ISBN 1 85391 069 4
Reprinted 1993, 1994, 1995 (Twice), 1996

A catalogue record for this book is available from the British Library.

Managing Editor Heather Dewhurst
Edited by Diana Brinton
Designed by Maggie Aldred
Photography by Debbie Patterson
Illustrations by John Hutchinson
Typesetting by BMD Graphics, Hemel Hempstead
Colour separation by Fotographics Limited, UK – Hong Kong
Printed in Hong Kong by Wing King Tong

Merehurst is the leading publisher of craft books and has an excellent range of titles to suit all levels. Please send to the address above for our free catalogue, stating the title of this book.

CONTENTS

INTRODUCTION

Samplers have been part of our way of life for several hundreds of years, but perhaps only became popular as decorative pieces of work in the 19th century, when they came to be used in this way by the Victorians. Originally, samplers were worked on evenweave linen, but as you will see from this book, they can look equally attractive embroidered on modern fabrics such as Zweigart's Aida.

A sampler provided a record of stitches and patterns worked in embroidery, and acted as a reference for the needlewoman's future projects. As well as stitches and patterns, traditional motifs and alphabets were added, together with personal touches, such as the name of the embroiderer and the date the sampler was completed. This book brings the sampler right up to date, while continuing the traditional theme in the use of alphabets and motifs.

Cross stitch is one of the oldest, and simplest, of all embroidery stitches. With the help of the instructions on this and the following pages, even complete beginners will find that many of these designs, such as the two small samplers, are well within their scope. Other projects, such as the traditional sampler, with its matching pictures, use a wide range of colours for shaded effects and will challenge more experienced embroiderers.

Whatever you choose to celebrate in cross stitch you will surely find a design suitable for the occasion, and you will create an heirloom for the future.

BASIC SKILLS

BEFORE YOU BEGIN

PREPARING THE FABRIC
Even with an average amount of handling, many evenweave fabrics tend to fray at the edges, so it is a good idea to overcast the raw edges, using ordinary sewing thread, before you begin.

THE INSTRUCTIONS
Each project begins with a full list of the materials that you will require. All the designs are worked on evenweave fabrics or Aida, produced by Zweigart. The measurements given for the embroidery fabric include a minimum of 5cm (2in) all around, to allow for stretching it in a frame and preparing the edges to prevent them from fraying.

Colour keys for stranded embroidery cottons – DMC, Anchor or Madeira – are given with each chart. It is assumed that you will need to buy one skein of each colour mentioned in a particular key even though you may use less, but where two or more skeins are needed, this information is included in the main list of requirements.

To work from the charts, particularly those where several symbols are used in close proximity, some readers may find it helpful to have the chart enlarged so that the squares and symbols can be seen more easily. Many photocopying services will do this for a minimum charge.

Before you begin to embroider, always mark the centre of the design with two lines of basting stitches, one vertical and one horizontal, running from edge to edge of the fabric, as indicated by the arrows on the charts.

As you stitch, use the centre lines given on the chart and the basting threads on your fabric as reference points for counting the squares and threads to position your design accurately.

WORKING IN A HOOP
A hoop is the most popular frame for use with small areas of embroidery. It consists of two rings, one fitted inside the other; the outer ring usually has an adjustable screw attachment so that it can be tightened to hold the stretched fabric in place.

Hoops are available in several sizes, ranging from 10cm (4in) in diameter to quilting hoops with a diameter of 38cm (15in). Hoops with table stands or floor stands attached are also available.

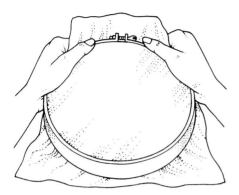

1 To stretch your fabric in a hoop, place the area to be embroidered over the inner ring and press the outer ring over it, with the tension screw released. Tissue paper can be placed between the outer ring and the embroidery, so that the hoop does not mark the fabric. Lay the tissue paper over the fabric when you set it in the hoop, then tear away the central embroidery area.

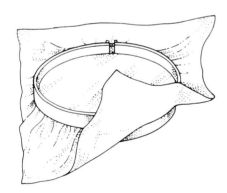

2 Smooth the fabric and, if necessary, straighten the grain before tightening the screw. The fabric should be evenly stretched.

WORKING IN A RECTANGULAR FRAME

Rectangular frames are more suitable for larger pieces of embroidery. They consist of two rollers, with tapes attached, and two flat side pieces, which slot into the rollers and are held in place by pegs or screw attachments. Available in different sizes, either alone or with adjustable table or floor stands, frames are measured by the length of the roller

tape, and range in size from 30cm (12in) to 68cm (27in).

As alternatives to a slate frame, canvas stretchers and the backs of old picture frames can be used. Provided there is sufficient extra fabric around the finished size of the embroidery, the edges can be turned under and simply attached with drawing pins (thumb tacks) or staples.

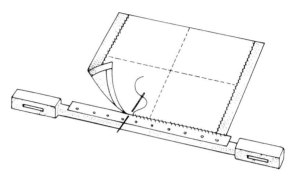

1 To stretch your fabric in a rectangular frame, cut out the fabric, allowing at least an extra 5cm (2in) all around the finished size of the embroidery. Baste a single 12mm (½in) turning on the top and bottom edges and oversew strong tape, 2.5cm (1in) wide, to the other two sides. Mark the centre line both ways with basting stitches. Working from the centre outward and using strong thread, oversew the top and bottom edges to the roller tapes. Fit the side pieces into the slotes, and roll any extra fabric on one roller until the fabric is taut.

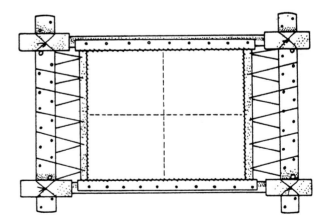

2 Insert the pegs or adjust the screw attachments to secure the frame. Thread a large-eyed needle (chenile needle) with strong thread or fine string and lace both edges, securing the ends around the intersections of the frame. Lace the webbing at 2.5cm (1in) intervals, stretching the fabric evenly.

EXTENDING EMBROIDERY FABRIC

It is easy to extend a piece of embroidery fabric, such as a bookmark, to stretch it in a hoop.

● Fabric oddments of a similar weight can be used. Simply cut four pieces to size (in other words, to the measurement that will fit both the embroidery fabric and your hoop) and baste them to each side of the embroidery fabric before stretching it in the hoop in the usual way.

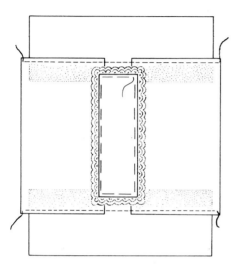

TO MITRE A CORNER

Press a single hem to the wrong side, the same as the measurement given in the instructions. Open the hem out again and fold the corner of the fabric inwards as shown on the diagram. Refold the hem to the wrong side along the pressed line, and slip-stitch in place.

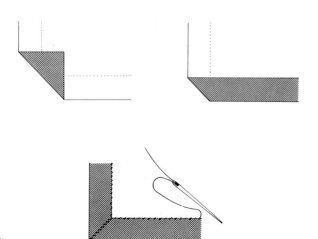

MOUNTING EMBROIDERY

The cardboard should be cut to the size of the finished embroidery, with an extra 6mm (¼in) added all round to allow for the recess in the frame.

LIGHTWEIGHT FABRICS

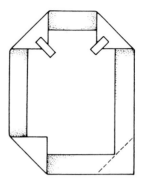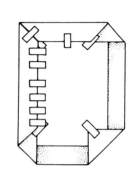

1 Place embroidery face down, with the cardboard centred on top, and basting and pencil lines matching. Begin by folding over the fabric at each corner and securing it with masking tape.

2 Working first on one side and then the other, fold over the fabric on all sides and secure it firmly with pieces of masking tape, placed about 2.5cm (1in) apart. Also neaten the mitred corners with masking tape, pulling the fabric tightly to give a firm, smooth finish.

HEAVIER FABRICS

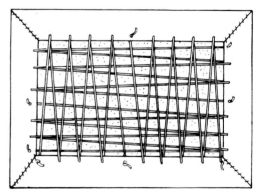

● Lay the embroidery face down, with the cardboard centred on top; fold over the edges of the fabric on opposite sides, making mitred folds at the corners, and lace across, using strong thread. Repeat on the other two sides. Finally, pull up the fabric firmly over the cardboard. Overstitch the mitred corners.

CROSS STITCH

For all cross stitch embroidery, the following two methods of working are used. In each case, neat rows of vertical stitches are produced on the back of the fabric.

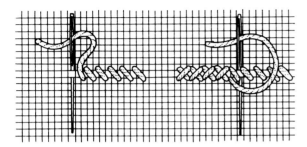

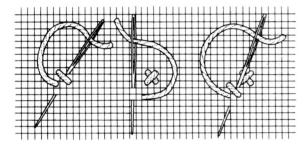

● When stitching large areas, work in horizontal rows. Working from right to left, complete the first row of evenly spaced diagonal stitches over the number of threads specified in the project instructions. Then, working from left to right, repeat the process. Continue in this way, making sure each stitch crosses in the same direction.

● When stitching diagonal lines, work downwards, completing each stitch before moving to the next. When starting a project always begin to embroider at the centre of the design and work outwards to ensure that the design will be placed centrally on the fabric.

FRENCH KNOTS

This stitch is shown on some of the diagrams by a small dot. Where there are several french knots, the dots have been omitted to avoid confusion. Where this occurs you should refer to the instructions of the project and the colour photograph.

To work a french knot, bring your needle and cotton out slightly to the right of where you want your knot to be. Wind the thread once or twice around the needle, depending on how big you want your knot to be, and insert the needle to the left of the point where you brought it out.

Be careful not to pull too hard or the knot will disappear through the fabric. The instructions state the number of strands of cotton to be used for the french knots.

BACKSTITCH

Backstitch is used in the projects to give emphasis to a particular foldline, an outline or a shadow. The stitches are worked over the same number of threads as the cross stitch, forming continuous straight or diagonal lines.

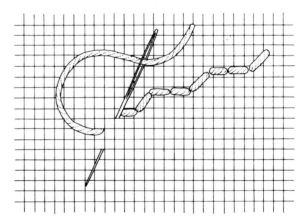

● Make the first stitch from left to right; pass the needle behind the fabric and bring it out one stitch length ahead to the left. Repeat and continue in this way along the line.

ADDING NAMES AND DATES

First of all, on a spare piece of graph paper, draw your names and dates, using the alphabet given for that particular project. Count the number of stitches in the width of each name or date and mark the centre. When you have done this draw the names and dates again, matching the centres with the centre of the sampler.

26th APRIL
1993

SUZANNE
♥
DAVID

Wedding Bells

A wedding is a great family occasion, so why not add your congratulations in cross stitch with a beautiful wedding sampler? Stitched on white evenweave linen, the shades of pink, peach and blue are perfect for the profusion of flowers and ribbons that make up the border. The hearts surrounding the names are a reminder of the love and affection the couple share.

WEDDING BELLS

YOU WILL NEED

For the Wedding Bells sampler, with a design area measuring 24cm × 25cm (9½in × 10in), or 124 stitches by 129 stitches, here in a frame measuring 36cm × 38cm (14½in × 15¼in):

34cm × 35cm (13½in × 14in) of white Lugana fabric, with 25 threads to 2.5cm (1in)
Stranded embroidery cotton in the colours given in the panel
No24 tapestry needle
Strong thread, for lacing across the back
Cardboard for mounting, sufficient to fit into the frame recess
Frame of your choice

●

THE EMBROIDERY

Prepare the fabric and stretch it in a frame as explained on page 5. Following the chart, start the embroidery at the centre of the design, using two strands of embroidery cotton in the needle. Work each stitch over two threads of fabric in each direction. Make sure that all the top crosses run in the same direction and that each row is worked into the same holes as the top or bottom of the row before, so that you do not leave a space between the rows.

With backstitch and using one strand of dark grey cotton, outline the bells and flowers, then embroider the date, month and year with two strands of dark grey cotton. The flower stalks are worked with two strands of medium green cotton in backstitch. Instructions for using an alphabet to write your own name and date are at the beginning of the book.

Work the centres of the blue flowers with french knots in light peach cotton.

MAKING UP

Gently steam press the work on the wrong side and mount it as explained on page 6. Choose an appropriate frame and mount to add the final touch to this record of a very special day.

WEDDING BELLS ▶		DMC	ANCHOR	MADEIRA
⊡	Light pink	3689	66	0606
⊞	Dark pink	3688	68	0605
⊟	Light mauve	211	108	0801
⋌	Dark mauve	210	109	0803
✳	Light peach	353	9	0304
⊿	Dark peach	758	9575	0403
⊺	Light blue	800	128	0908
⊙	Medium blue	799	130	0910
◼	Dark blue	798	131	0911
⊓	Light green	3348	264	1409
⊠	Medium green	3052	844	1509
▲	Dark green	936	263	1507
◇	Light grey	415	398	1803
◼	Dark grey	414	399	1801

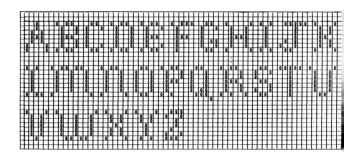

Home Sweet Home

The traditional text of this *Home Sweet Home* sampler, embellished with a striking border, will help to make your house a home.
The sampler uses a spectrum of sumptuous jewel shades – jade and emerald greens, pinks and purples – to complement the composition and create a vivid embroidery. The pattern of the deep border is richly resplendent, making the perfect frame for the traditional-style lettering.

HOME SWEET HOME

YOU WILL NEED

For the Home Sweet Home sampler, with a design area measuring 23cm (9in) square, or 125 stitches each way, here in a frame measuring 36cm (14½in) square:

33cm (13in) square of Zweigart's white, 14-count Aida fabric
Stranded embroidery cotton in the colours given in the panel
No24 tapestry needle
Strong thread, for lacing across the back
Cardboard, for mounting, sufficient to fit into the frame recess
Frame of your choice

•

THE EMBROIDERY

Prepare the fabric and stretch it in a frame as explained on page 5. Following the chart, start the embroidery at the centre of the design, using two strands of embroidery cotton in the needle. Work each stitch over one block of fabric in each direction, making sure that all the top crosses run in the same direction and each row is worked into the same holes as the top or bottom of the row before, so that you do not leave a space between the rows. For a simple sampler, the words 'Home Sweet Home' could be worked with just the inner border around the outside and for the finishing touch, you might add a row of stitching in dark magenta one square away from the inner border.

MAKING UP

Gently steam press the work on the wrong side and mount it as explained on page 6. Choose your own mount and frame from the large selection available in the shops or use one of the many framing services available to put the finishing touch to your work.

HOME SWEET HOME ▶		DMC	ANCHOR	MADEIRA
:	Light pink	776	73	0606
%	Dark pink	899	40	0609
>	Light mauve	3608	86	0709
+	Dark mauve	718	88	0707
v	Yellow	743	301	0113
X	Light green	320	215	1310
−	Medium green	367	216	1312
s	Dark green	319	217	1313

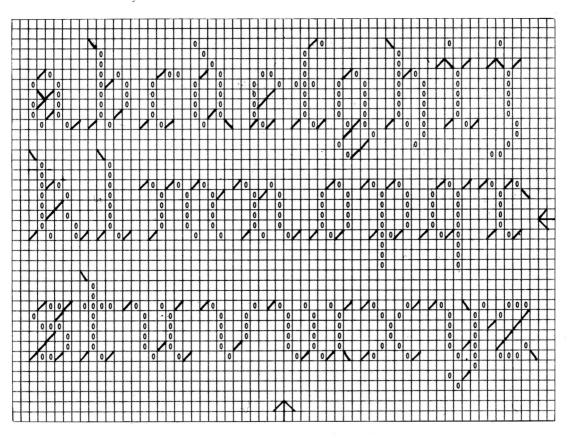

Alternative alphabet

Bordered Alphabet

The treatment of traditional motifs and an alphabet in pastel colours bring this sampler up to date. The border of carnations can easily be extended to make space for your own words underneath the alphabet, or perhaps you could use the space filled here by the letters of the alphabet to write your own message.

This sampler can easily be adapted by using alternative shades of cotton. You might choose the opulence of rich, deeper shades, for example, or select colours to match your decor.

BORDERED ALPHABET

YOU WILL NEED

For the Bordered Alphabet sampler, with a design area measuring 26cm × 15cm (10¼in × 6in), or 144 stitches by 85 stitches, here in a frame measuring 36cm × 25cm (14½in × 10in):

36cm × 25cm (14in × 10in) of Zweigart's cream, 14-count Aida fabric
Stranded embroidery cotton in the colours given in the panel
No24 tapestry needle
Strong thread, for lacing across the back
Cardboard, for mounting, sufficient to fit into the frame recess
Frame of your choice

•

THE EMBROIDERY

Prepare the fabric and stretch it in a frame as explained on page 5. Following the chart, start the embroidery at the centre of the design, using two strands of embroidery cotton in the needle. Work each stitch over one block of fabric in each direction. Make sure that all the top crosses run in the same direction and that each row is worked into the same holes as the top or bottom of the row before so that you do not leave a space between the rows.

MAKING UP

Gently steam press the work on the wrong side and mount it as explained on page 6. Choose a mount and frame to complement your embroidery colours.

BORDERED ALPHABET ▶		DMC	ANCHOR	MADEIRA
‡	Light pink	3689	66	0606
–	Dark pink	3688	68	0605
o	Pale magenta	3609	85	0710
s	Light mauve	211	108	0801
x	Dark mauve	210	109	0803
‹	Light green	369	213	1309
=	Dark green	368	214	1310
%	Brown	841	378	1911

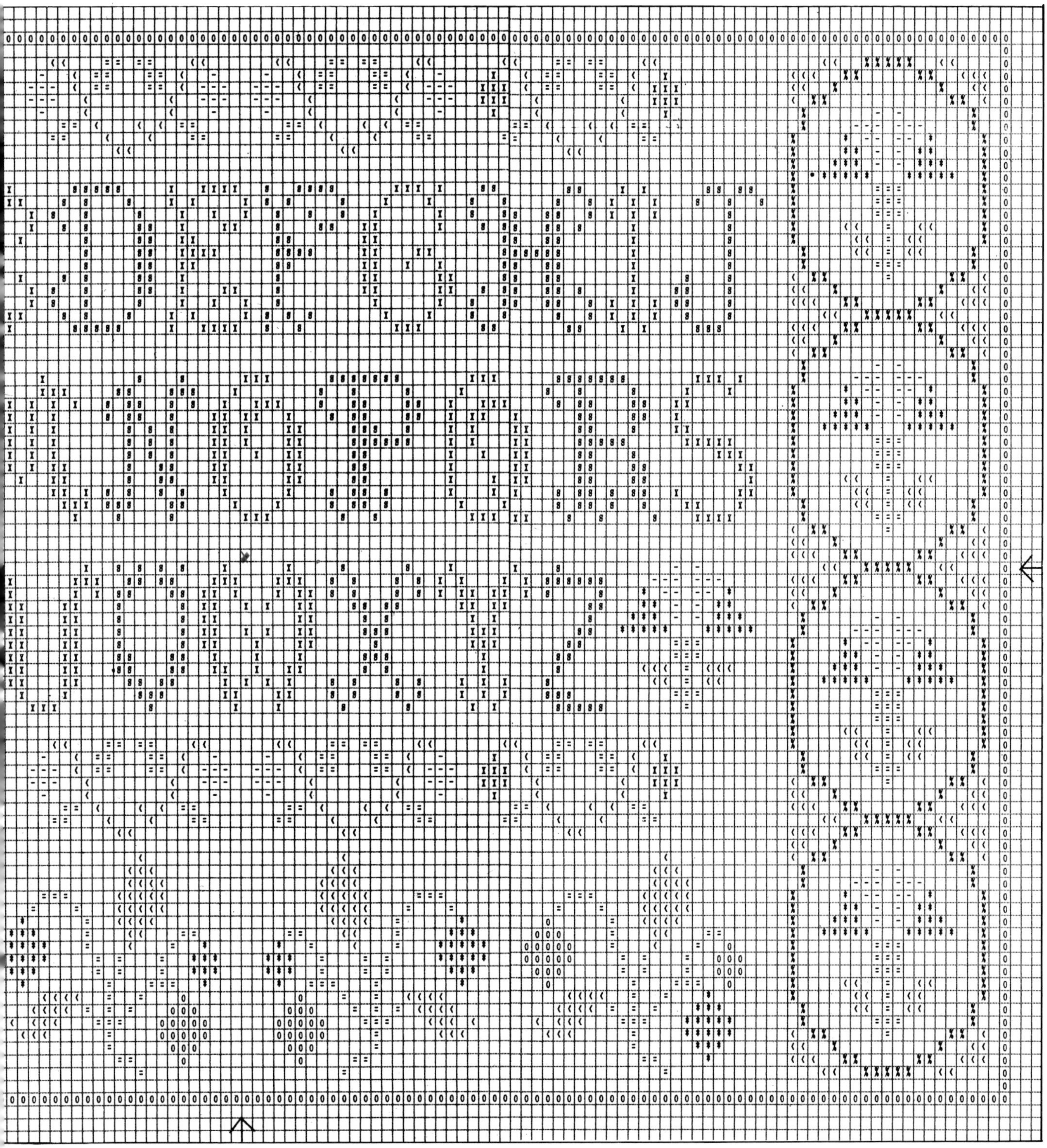

Samplers for Children

A new baby! Record the excitement, laughter, joy and celebration in a lovingly-stitched birth sampler. In the first design, two slender storks, encircled by a heart, hold a bouquet over the baby's name and date of birth. This sampler is worked in soft shades – pastel colours to echo those tender feelings a new baby rouses in every heart.

The motif sampler makes full use of a paint-box palette and appealing images to create a bright, bold design. Motifs carefully chosen for their childhood charm surround the baby's name and birthdate. The delightful duck and teddy are stitched separately as matching pictures.

SAMPLERS FOR CHILDREN

YOU WILL NEED

For each of the designs – Stork, Motif, Duck and Teddy – you will need the following, plus the individual requirements specified below:

Stranded embroidery cotton in the colours given in the appropriate panel
No24 tapestry needle
Strong thread, for lacing across the back
Cardboard, for mounting, sufficient to fit into the frame recess
Frame of your choice

For the Stork sampler, with a design area measuring 16cm × 20cm (6¼in × 8in), or 89 stitches by 114 stitches, here in a frame measuring 25cm × 30cm (10in × 12in):

26cm × 30cm (10¼in × 12in) of Zweigart's white, 14-count Aida fabric

For the Motif sampler, with a design area measuring 20cm × 15cm (8in × 6in), or 112 stitches by 86 stitches, here in a frame measuring 32cm × 27.5cm (12¾in × 11in):

30cm × 25cm (12in × 10in) of Zweigart's white, 14-count Aida fabric

For the Duck picture, with a design area measuring 6.5cm × 6cm (2½in × 2¼in), or 36 stitches by 35 stitches, here in a frame measuring 17cm (6¾in) square:

13cm × 12cm (5in × 4½in) of Zweigart's white, 14-count Aida fabric

For the Teddy picture, with a design area measuring 7cm × 6.5cm (2¾in × 2½in), or 38 stitches by 36 stitches, here in a frame measuring 17cm (6¾in) square:

14cm × 13cm (5½in × 5in) of Zweigart's white, 14-count Aida fabric

THE EMBROIDERY

In each case, prepare the fabric and stretch it in a frame (see page 5). Following the appropriate chart, start at the centre of the design, using two strands of cotton in the needle. Work each stitch over one block of fabric in each direction. Make sure that all top crosses run in the same direction and that each row is worked into the same holes as the top or bottom of the row before, so that you do not leave a space between rows.

For the Stork sampler, embroider the leaf stems with two strands of green cotton and the bow with two strands of dark pink cotton. Outline the heart and the storks, and embroider the feet, name and date with one strand of dark brown cotton. If you are making the sampler for a boy, you might choose to embroider the flowers in blue rather than pink.

For the Motif sampler and pictures, the motifs are outlined in backstitch with one strand of dark grey cotton, and the date and ladybird legs are worked with two strands of dark grey. The duck's eye is a single french knot in dark grey cotton.

MAKING UP

Gently steam press the finished embroideries on the wrong side and mount them as explained on page 6. When choosing the mounts and frames, consider the colour scheme of the room, as the set of pictures will make a striking and attractive feature.

STORK ▶		DMC	ANCHOR	MADEIRA
+	Cream	746	275	0101
o	Light pink	3689	66	0606
s	Dark pink	3688	68	0605
‡	Green	368	214	1310
‹	Light brown	842	376	1910
=	Dark brown	840	679	1912

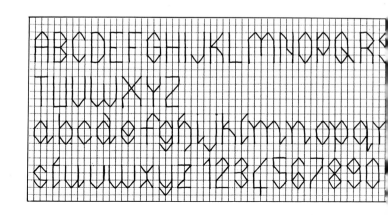

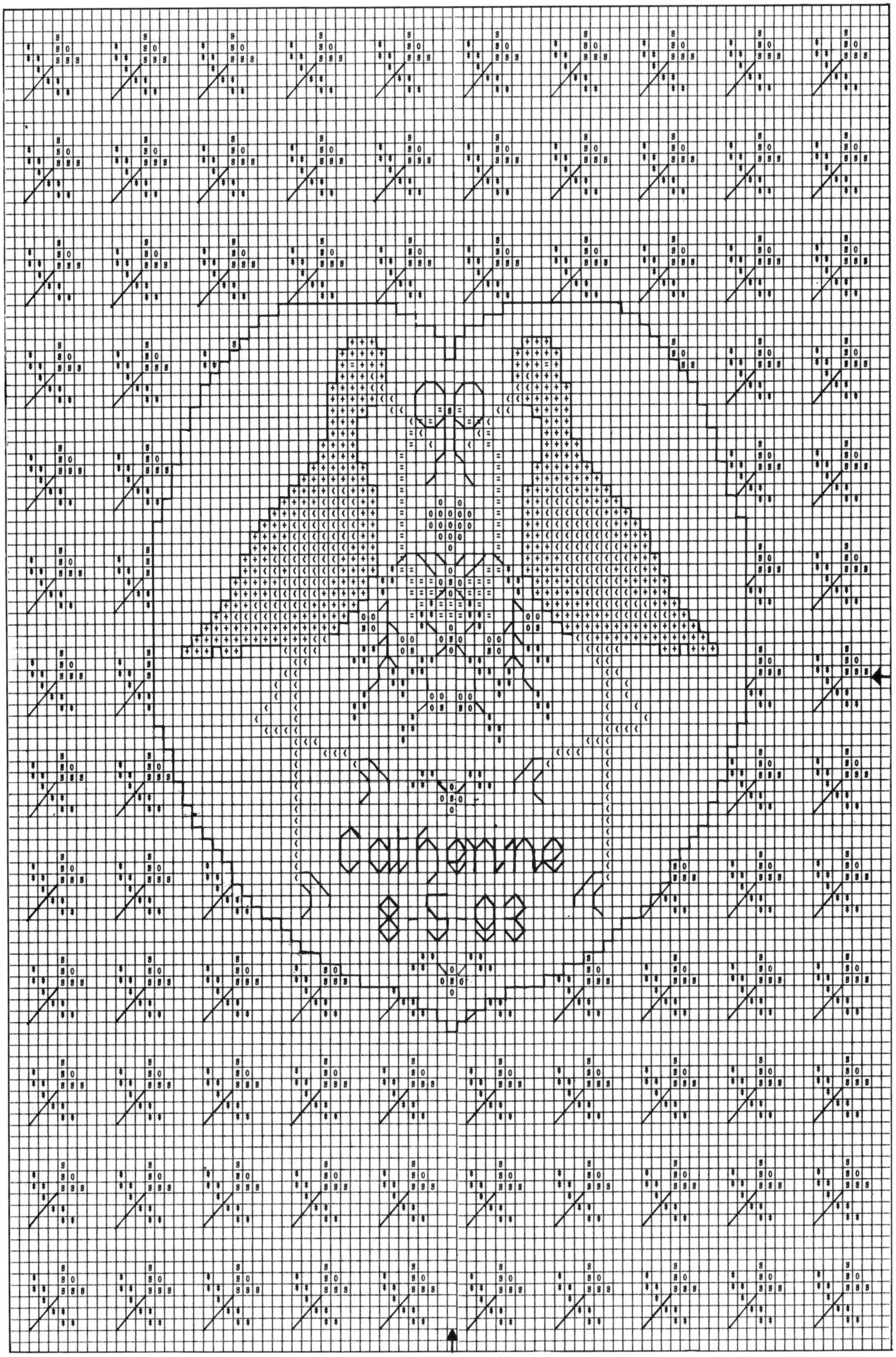
Catherine
8-5-93

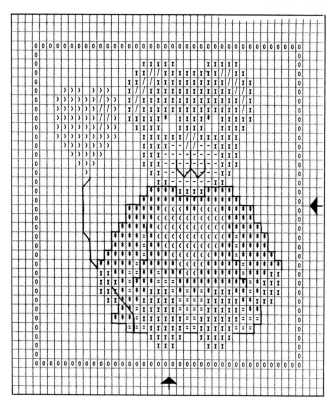

TEDDY ▲		DMC	ANCHOR	MADEIRA
/	Light pink	3689	66	0606
<	Dark pink	3688	68	0605
)	Dark mauve	208	111	0804
−	Gold	676	887	2208
‡	Light blue	800	128	0908
=	Dark blue	799	130	0910
x	Brown	434	365	2009
o	Light grey	415	398	1803
	Dark grey*	414	399	1801

Note: dark grey* is used for bks outline.

DUCK ▲		DMC	ANCHOR	MADEIRA
c	Cream	746	275	0101
/	Light pink	3689	66	0606
<	Dark pink	3688	68	0605
v	Yellow	3078	292	0102
r	Green	3348	264	1409
o	Light grey	415	398	1803
	Dark grey*	414	399	1801

Note: dark blue (see Motif Sampler) used for eye only; dark grey* is used for bks outline.

MOTIF SAMPLER ▶		DMC	ANCHOR	MADEIRA
c	Cream	746	275	0101
/	Light pink	3689	66	0606
<	Dark pink	3688	68	0605
\	Light mauve	210	109	0803
)	Dark mauve	208	111	0804
+	Crimson	309	42	0510
v	Yellow	3078	292	0102
−	Gold	676	887	2208
‡	Light blue	800	128	0908
=	Dark blue	799	130	0910
r	Green	3348	264	1409
x	Brown	434	365	2009
o	Light grey	415	398	1803
	Dark grey*	414	399	1801

Note: dark grey* is used for bks outline.

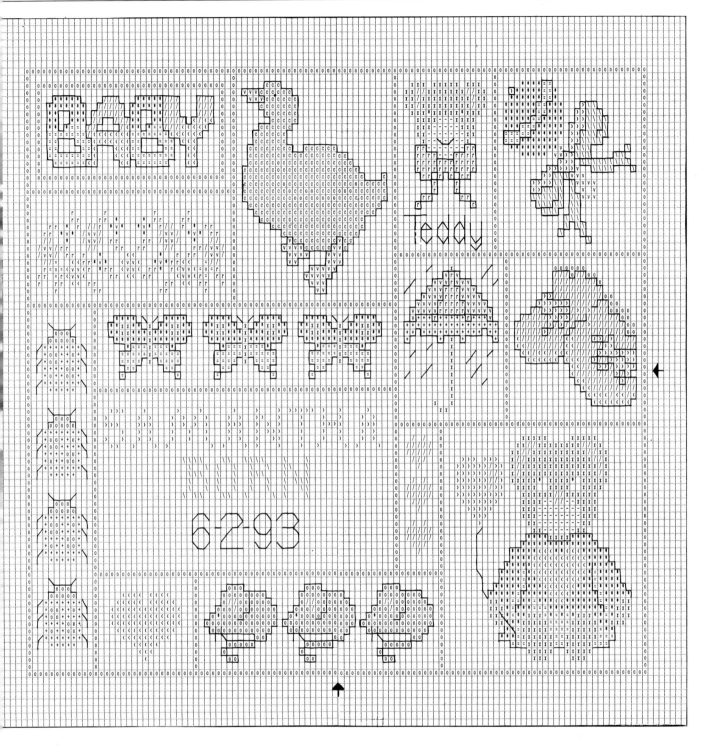

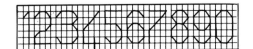

Small and Beautiful

These little samplers make an excellent introduction to cross stitch. The projects are small, and quick to complete, but provide the stitcher with an attractive first embroidery.

SMALL AND BEAUTIFUL

YOU WILL NEED

For Love is Kind, with a design area measuring 14.5cm × 17.5cm (5¾in × 7in), or 81 stitches by 97 stitches, here in a frame measuring 27cm × 30cm (10¾in × 12in):

24cm × 28cm (9½in × 11in) of Zweigart's cream, 14-count Aida fabric
Stranded embroidery cotton in the colours given in the appropriate panel
No24 tapestry needle
Strong thread, for lacing across the back
Cardboard, for mounting, sufficient to fit into the frame recess
Frame of your choice

For Home Sweet Home, with a design area measuring 17.5cm × 14cm (7in × 5½in), or 97 stitches by 77 stitches, here in a frame measuring 30.5cm × 26cm (12¼in × 10½in):

28cm × 24cm (11in × 9½in) of Zweigart's cream, 14-count Aida fabric
Stranded embroidery cotton in the colours given in the appropriate panel
No24 tapestry needle
Strong thread, for lacing across the back
Cardboard, for mounting, sufficient to fit into the frame recess
Frame of your choice

THE EMBROIDERY

Prepare the fabric and stretch it in a frame as explained on page 5. Following the appropriate chart, start the embroidery at the centre of the design, using two strands of embroidery cotton in the needle. Work each stitch over one block of fabric in each direction. Make sure that all the top crosses run in the same direction and that each row is worked into the same holes as the top or bottom of the row before so that you do not leave a space between the rows.

The bow and stalks on the *Love is Kind* sampler are worked in backstitch with two strands of green cotton, and the roses on the *Home Sweet Home* sampler are outlined with one strand of dark green cotton.

MAKING UP

Gently steam press the work on the wrong side and mount it as explained on page 6. The samplers could be framed as a matching pair or as two separate projects. The pine frames seen here complement the soft peach shades used for the embroideries, but these gentle shades could be exchanged for more vibrant colours to give a stronger feel to the designs.

Both samplers would look equally attractive stitched on an 11-count Aida fabric, which is particularly easy for a beginner to use. Remember that you may need extra stranded cotton for a design worked on an 11-count Aida because the stitches are bigger.

The *Love is Kind* sampler could be used as a small wedding sampler if the initials of the bride and groom were added, together with the date.

HOME SWEET HOME ◀		DMC	ANCHOR	MADEIRA
=	Pink	3688	68	0605
‹	Light peach	353	9	0304
+	Dark peach	352	10	0303
s	Light green	3052	844	1509
x	Dark green	319	218	1313
%	Brown	640	393	1905

LOVE IS KIND ▶		DMC	ANCHOR	MADEIRA
c	Ecru	Ecru	926	Ecru
‹	Light peach	758	9575	0403
+	Dark peach	352	10	0303
x	Green	368	214	1310
%	Light brown	841	378	1911
=	Dark brown	829	906	2106

Traditional Sampler

This sampler would have looked perfectly at home hanging in a Victorian parlour around the turn of the century. A selection of traditional motifs of flowers and birds have been arranged to make this attractive design. Three of the motifs have been embroidered separately to make a delightful trio of pictures, or perhaps you would like to create a bell pull from the motifs, giving a truly Victorian flavour to your decor.

TRADITIONAL SAMPLER

YOU WILL NEED

For the sampler and each of the small pictures derived from it, you will need the following, plus the individual requirements specified below:

Stranded embroidery cotton in the colours given in the appropriate panel
No24 tapestry needle
Strong thread, for lacing across the back
Cardboard, for mounting, sufficient to fit into the frame recess
Frame of your choice

For the sampler, with a design area measuring 34cm × 25.5cm (13½in × 10¼in), or 183 stitches by 138 stitches, here in a frame measuring 40cm × 32.5cm (16in × 13in):

44cm × 35cm (17½in × 14in) of cream Linda fabric, with 27 threads to 2.5cm (1in)

For the Rose picture, with a design area measuring 12cm × 13cm (4½in × 5in), or 64 stitches by 70 stitches, here in a frame measuring 18.5cm (7½in) square:

22cm × 23cm (8½in × 9in) of cream Linda fabric, with 27 threads to 2.5cm (1in)

For the Cornflower picture, with a design area measuring 15cm × 11cm (6in × 4¼in), or 83 stitches by 59 stitches, here in a frame measuring 21cm × 16.5cm (8¼in × 6½in):

25cm × 21cm (10in × 8¼in) of cream Linda fabric, with 27 threads to 2.5cm (1in)

34   CHART 1

For the Bird picture, with a design area measuring 11cm × 8cm (4¼in × 3in), or 59 stitches by 44 stitches, here in a frame measuring 16.5cm × 13.5cm (6½in × 5¼in):

21cm × 18cm (8¼in × 7¼in) of cream Linda fabric, with 27 threads to 2.5cm (1in)

•

THE EMBROIDERY

For each design, prepare the linen and stretch in a frame as explained on page 5. Following the chart, start the embroidery at the centre of the design, using two strands of embroidery cotton in the needle. Embroider each stitch over two threads of fabric in each direction. Make sure that all the top crosses run in the same direction and each row is worked into the same holes as the row before so

that you do not leave a space between the rows. Work the butterfly feelers with two strands of dark brown cotton in backstitch.

MAKING UP

Gently steam press the work on the wrong side and mount it as explained on page 6. To retain the traditional feel of the sampler, choose a simple wooden frame without a cardboard mount.

NOTE

The sampler has been divided into four charts, each showing a quarter. The key and Charts 3 and 4 are on pages 38-9.

CHART 2

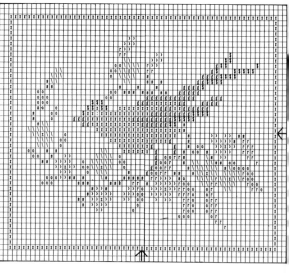

BIRD ▲		DMC	ANCHOR	MADEIRA
↘	Light mauve	341	117	0901
<	Dark mauve	340	118	0902
g	Gold	834	874	2204
z	Dark yellow	725	298	0113
‡	Light blue	3325	976	1002
o	Light green	471	265	1502
r	Medium green	988	244	1402
s	Dark green	986	246	1404
x	Light brown	612	832	2002
$	Dark brown	370	856	2201

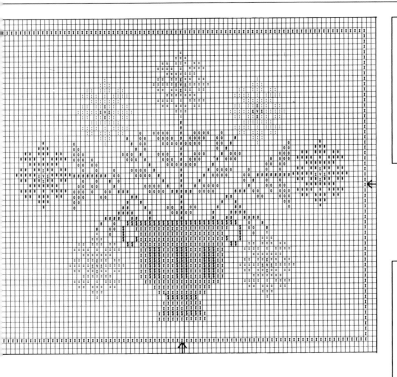

CORNFLOWER ◄		DMC	ANCHOR	MADEIRA
v	Light yellow	727	293	0110
z	Dark yellow	725	306	0108
‡	Light blue	3325	976	1002
:	Medium blue	334	977	1003
=	Dark blue	312	979	1005
o	Light green	471	265	1502
s	Dark green	986	246	1404
x	Light brown	612	832	2002
$	Dark brown	370	856	2201

ROSE ▼		DMC	ANCHOR	MADEIRA
%	Pale magenta	3609	85	0710
v	Light yellow	727	295	0111
z	Dark yellow	725	298	0113
o	Light green	471	265	1502
r	Medium green	988	244	1402
s	Dark green	986	246	1404
x	Light brown	612	832	2002
$	Dark brown	370	856	2201

37

CHART 3

CHART 1	CHART 2
CHART 3	CHART 4

CHART 4

Butterflies

Decorated with butterflies, this
sampler reminds one of sunny
summer skies. The bright shades of
pink in the centre are echoed in the
floral border to continue the theme.
Once again, part of the design could
be omitted to add that personal touch.
Your finished sampler will be like a
breath of fresh air lifting the spirits.
Stitch a feast for the eyes and
revel in it!

BUTTERFLIES

YOU WILL NEED

For the Butterflies sampler, with a design area measuring 22cm × 17.5cm (8½in × 7in), or 119 stitches by 97 stitches, here in a frame measuring 34cm × 30cm (13½in × 12in):

32cm × 27.5cm (12¾in × 11in) of Zweigart's white, 14-count Aida fabric
Stranded embroidery cotton in the colours given in the panel
No24 tapestry needle
Strong thread, for lacing across the back
Cardboard, for mounting, sufficient to fit into the frame recess
Frame of your choice

●

THE EMBROIDERY

Prepare the fabric and stretch it in a frame as explained on page 5. Following the chart, start the embroidery at the centre of the design, using two strands of embroidery cotton in the needle. Work each stitch over one block of fabric in each direction. Make sure that all the top crosses run in the same direction and each row is worked into the same holes as the top or bottom of the row before so that you do not leave a space between the rows.

Work the butterfly feelers in dark brown cotton, backstitching over two blocks of fabric.

MAKING UP

Gently steam press the work on the wrong side and mount it as explained on page 6. As this sampler has a rather bright modern feel about it, one of the floral-type frames might look attractive.

BUTTERFLIES ▶	DMC	ANCHOR	MADEIRA
% Light pink	605	50	0613
+ Dark pink	602	63	0702
✗ Yellow	3078	292	0102
c Light blue	932	920	1602
s Dark blue	311	148	1007
∕ Light green	3052	844	1509
: Dark green	3051	845	1508
= Light brown	841	378	1911
⟩ Dark brown	640	393	1905

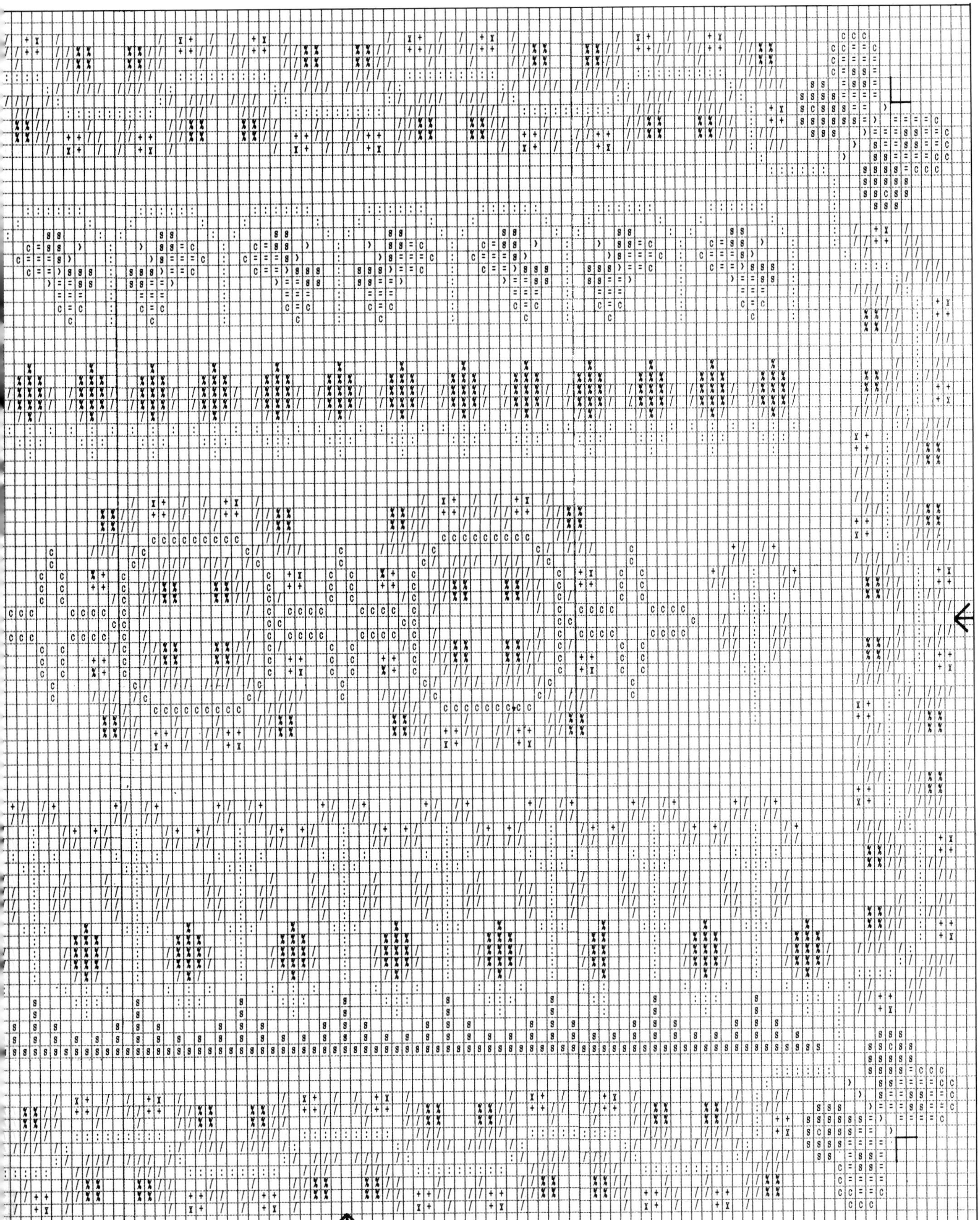

Floral Feast

Once again, a selection of traditional flower motifs have been arranged to create this attractive floral sampler. The pinks in the basket of roses are echoed in the daisy-like flowers at the top of the sampler and complement the mauve shades of the other flowers. By adding your name and the date the sampler was worked, you can create an heirloom for future generations!

FLORAL FEAST

YOU WILL NEED

For the Floral Feast sampler, with a design area measuring 18.5cm × 21cm (7½in × 8¼in), or 101 stitches by 119 stitches, here in a frame measuring 31cm × 35cm (12¼in × 14in):

28.5cm × 31cm (11½in × 12¼in) of Zweigart's white, 14-count Aida fabric
Stranded embroidery cotton in the colours given in the panel
No24 tapestry needle
Strong thread, for lacing across the back
Cardboard, for mounting, sufficient to fit into the frame recess
Frame of your choice

•

THE EMBROIDERY

Prepare the fabric and stretch it in a frame as explained on page 5. Following the appropriate chart, start the embroidery at the centre of the design, using two strands of embroidery cotton in the needle. Work each stitch over one block of fabric in each direction. Make sure that all the top crosses run in the same direction and each row is worked into the same holes as the top or bottom of the row before so that you do not leave a space between the rows.

Embroider your name and the date, following the instructions on page 7.

MAKING UP

Gently steam press the work on the wrong side and mount it as explained on page 6. As this is a sampler with traditional motifs, it has been framed without a mount so that it is in keeping with the samplers stitched around the turn of the century. The rose motif would look most attractive as a separate picture, and other motifs could also be extracted and used in this manner, perhaps with minor modifications.

FLORAL FEAST ▶		DMC	ANCHOR	MADEIRA
‹	Light pink	604	60	0614
+	Medium pink	603	63	0701
o	Dark pink	600	65	0704
%	Light mauve	210	108	0803
–	Dark mauve	208	111	0804
v	Yellow	743	301	0113
s	Light green	369	213	1309
=	Medium green	320	215	1311
‡	Dark green	367	217	1312
x	Light brown	729	890	2209
›	Dark brown	434	365	2009

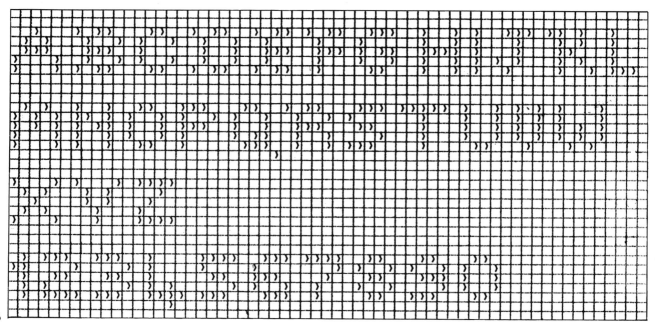

ACKNOWLEDGEMENTS

The author would like to thank the following people for their help with projects in this book:

Kate Riley, Jenny Thorpe, Lyn Freeman, Cilla King, Diane Teal and especially Helen Burke.

Thanks are also due to DMC Creative World Ltd, for supplying fabrics and threads, Mike Grey at Framecraft Miniatures Limited for the table linen, box and picture frame, and the staff of Speedframe at 140 High Street, Lincoln, for their excellent framing service.

Embroidery kits designed by Jane Alford may be obtained from her company:

Reflexions,
The Stables,
Black Bull Yard,
Welton,
Lincoln LN2 3HZ

SUPPLIERS

The following mail order company has supplied some of the basic items needed for making up the projects in this book:

Framecraft Miniatures Limited
148-150 High Street
Aston
Birmingham, B6 4US
England
Telephone (021) 359 4442

Addresses for Framecraft stockists worldwide
Ireland Needlecraft Pty. Ltd.
2-4 Keppel Drive
Hallam, Victoria 3803
Australia

Danish Art Needlework
PO Box 442, Lethbridge
Alberta T1J 3Z1
Canada

Sanyei Imports
PO Box 5, Hashima Shi
Gifu 501-62
Japan

The Embroidery Shop
286 Queen Street
Masterton
New Zealand

Anne Brinkley Designs Inc.
246 Walnut Street
Newton
Mass. 02160
USA

S A Threads and Cottons Ltd.
43 Somerset Road
Cape Town
South Africa

For information on your nearest stockist of embroidery cotton, contact the following:

DMC

UK
DMC Creative World Limited
62 Pullman Road
Wigston
Leicester, LE8 2DY
Telephone: 0533 811040

USA
The DMC Corporation
Port Kearney Bld.
10 South Kearney
N.J. 07032-0650
Telephone: 201 589 0606

AUSTRALIA
DMC Needlecraft Pty
P.O. Box 317
Earlswood 2206
NSW 2204
Telephone: 02599 3088

COATS AND ANCHOR

UK
Kilncraigs Mill
Alloa
Clackmannanshire
Scotland, FK10 1EG
Telephone: 0259 723431

USA
Coats & Clark
P.O. Box 27067
Dept CO1
Greenville
SC 29616
Telephone: 803 234 0103

AUSTRALIA
Coats Patons Crafts
Thistle Street
Launceston
Tasmania 7250
Telephone: 00344 4222

MADEIRA

UK
Madeira Threads (UK) Limited
Thirsk Industrial Park
York Road, Thirsk
N. Yorkshire, YO7 3BX
Telephone: 0845 524880

U.S.A.
Madeira Marketing Limited
600 East 9th Street
Michigan City
IN 46360
Telephone: 219 873 1000

AUSTRALIA
Penguin Threads Pty Limited
25-27 Izett Street
Prahran
Victoria 3181
Telephone: 03529 4400